Old School ι.

100 COMMON QUESTIONS

A Guide to Understanding
Classical Christian Education

DR. TIMOTHY DERNLAN

Titus Books
Philadelphia, PA

Titus Books

100 Common Questions:
A Guide to Understanding Classical Christian Education

Version 1.1
© 2021 by Timothy Dernlan
ISBN: 979-8-54780-110-5

Contact Information:
Dr. Timothy Dernlan
www.timdernlan.com

1. Classical Christian Education   2. Classical Education
3. Latin Schools   4. Intentional Christian Education
5. Classical Christian Education Alliance

First Edition: August 2021

Printed in the United States of America

For Christ and Our Future

TABLE OF CONTENTS

INTRODUCTION
9

HISTORY
11

PHILOSOPHY
17

CHRISTIAN
25

CLASSICAL
33

32) What is *in loco parentis?* 33) Why is *truth, goodness, and beauty* a common phrase? 34) What is *multum non multa?* 35) *What is paideia?* 36) What is *ad fontes?* 37) What are the *seven liberal arts?* 38) *What is the Trivium?* 39) *What is the Quadrivium?* 40) What is meant by *plundering the Egyptians?* 41) *What is meant by Scholé in education?* 42) What is meant by *teaching students how to think not what to think?* 43) What is meant by *joining the great conversation?* 44) What does it mean to *cultivate virtue* in students? 45) What does the term *soul formation* mean? 46) What is *omnibus* in a curriculum? 47) What does *imago dei* mean? 48) What does *ex nihilo* mean? 49) What does *Soli Deo Gloria* mean? 50) What does the word *arete* mean?

GRAMMAR
43

51) Is Grammar a subject or a stage of education? 52) Why are songs, chants, and memorization so important? 53) Why do students memorize so many things? 54) Why is cursive taught? 55) Why is the study of Latin important? 56) Why is phonics used to learn reading? 57) Why is proper spelling emphasized? 58) Why do students study ancient history at such a young age?

LOGIC
49

59) Is Logic a subject or a stage of education? 60) Why is the study of logic so important? 61) Why are questions a major tool of teachers in the logic school? 62) Is it common for children to act rude or mean in logic school 63) Why is ancient history a focus of study? 64) Why is ancient literature a focus of study? 65) Why are false gods and mythology part of the curriculum? 66) Why is physical education required?

RHETORIC
55

67) Is Rhetoric a subject or a stage of education? 68) Why is art a required subject? 69) Why is music a required subject? 70) What is a house system? 71) Why is technology not emphasized? 72) What is Socratic Learning? 73) What is the role of athletics? 74) Are classical Christian schools weak in math and science? 75) Why is Greek a valuable language to study? 76) How are students trained in proper manners? 77) What is a senior thesis presentation?

PARENTING
61

GRADUATES
65

GOVERNMENT
69

QUOTES
73

CONCLUSION
77

REFERENCES
79

ABOUT THE AUTHOR
80

INTRODUCTION

The recent resurgence of classical Christian education has made it possible for about fifteen percent of American students attending a private school or homeschool to receive this excellent intentionally Christian form of education. If you are new to classical Christian education, "welcome to the family!" You are joining an amazing community with a rich tradition of wonderfully effective and time-tested education. For those of you reading this who have been in the movement for several decades, thank you for your service and work to blaze the trail for the rest of us to follow.

Most of the answers to the questions in this book will have great shared understanding throughout the classical Christian education movement. However, some questions will be answered in slightly different ways by well-respected veterans in the field. If your school, administrator, teacher, or friend answers some of these questions in different ways, it is a great opportunity to participate in a dialogue, or Socratic discussion, to work through the differences and become more unified in your approach to this high calling of education. This should be done to gain a deeper understanding of the true, good, and beautiful education we seek to provide our children.

I hope you enjoy this book and that it is helpful to your classical Christian education journey. Be sure to share it with a friend, discuss the ideas, and take action to advance excellence and understanding of classical Christian education in your local community. May God bless you, your family, and your school as you pursue excellence in classical Christian education.

HISTORY

1
What is the origin of classical education?

Classical education can be traced back to Plato's foundation of the Academy in Athens, Greece circa 385 B.C. Other philosophers in this same era such as Socrates, Aristotle, Epicurus, and Isocrates were also instrumental in the formation of educational ideals leading to classical education and the seven liberal arts. When the Roman military conquered the Greeks, the intellectual ideas and influence of Greek culture and education remained strong and were incorporated into the Roman way of life. Then, Quintilian, a Roman rhetorician born in 35 A.D., began the process of placing many Greek educational ideas into age-appropriate stages of learning and classical education was solidified.

2
How did classical Christian education emerge?

The educational ideas of Quintilian had an influence on many Christian theologians and scholars such as Origen, Ambrose, Jerome, and Augustine. In Confessions, St. Augustine presented the first fully formed explanation of Christian education circa 397 A.D. As the Bishop of Hippo, Augustine had a major influence on the Christian church and education of the youth. Augustine merged classical education with Christian education in his teachings and proclaimed the liberal arts as "proper nutriment of the soul." This merging of Christian education with classical pedagogy proved foundational and influential throughout Christendom.

3
Did classical Christian education exist in the Middle Ages?

The pattern of Christian classical education continued to grow during the Middle Ages. Classical methodology became the standard formula for educational instruction, but the writings of Cassiodorus, a Roman senator born in 480 A.D., uniquely merged Christian and classical education. His writings advanced and solidified classical Christian education as common practice for both Christian and non-Christian communities. In the sixth century, Boethius, a Christian scholar, split the seven liberal arts into two categories of the Trivium and Quadrivium. The Quadrivium was an addition to education in the Middle Ages, but the Trivium of grammar, logic, and rhetoric can be traced to both the Greeks and Romans.

4

Why does classical Christian education seem so new and different?

In the early 1900's the effects of modern philosophy created noticeable changes to the look and feel of education. Philosophers such as Rousseau (b. 1712), Hegel, (b. 1770), Dewey (b. 1859), Piaget (b. 1896), and others worked to dilute and remove Christianity from education. These seemingly subtle shifts in the late 1800's have created cavernous differences between modern schools and classical Christian schools. Modern schools are now child-centered rather than Christ-centered, and the doctrines of socially accepted morality have replaced objective standards of truth, goodness, and beauty found in God's Word. The final byproduct is felt in classroom curriculum, teaching methods, academic standards, and behavioral expectations.

5

What is the recent history of classical Christian education in America?

A few of the many individuals who had a major impact on the recent resurgence of classical Christian education include Dorthey Sayers (b. 1893), Mortimer Adler (b. 1902), and Douglas Wilson (b. 1953). In 1947, Sayers presented *The Lost Tools of Learning*, an essay challenging her audience to recover and reinstitute the trivium of classical education. Years later, Douglas Wilson read the essay and founded a Christian school seeking to follow her challenge. That school, and a book by Wilson entitled *Recovering the Lost Tools of Learning*, eventually led to the formation of the Association of Classical Christian Schools (ACCS). Mortimer Adler was another influential individual advocating for a return to classical education. He was the co-founder of the *Great Books Society*, served as a professor at the University of Chicago, and authored many books advancing classical education in the late 1900's.

6
What is the Association of Classical Christian Schools?

The Association of Classical Christian Schools (ACCS) is the largest organization of classical Christian schools in America. The ACCS has over 350 member schools and can be found in all 50 of the United States and several other countries. The ACCS is a Christ-centered network of schools that advances classical Christian education, provides an annual national conference, offers national Accreditation, and other member resources. The ACCS was founded in 1991 after Douglas Wilson's book, *Recovering the Lost Tools of Learning*, inspired many individuals to start classical Christian schools around the nation.

7
What are the major classical Christian school organizations in America?

More recently, there have been many more classical Christian school organizations founded to advance this great form of education. Below are several of the organizations and associations advancing classical Christian education in America.

Anglican School Association
Ambleside Schools
Association of Classical Christian Schools
Classical Christian Education Alliance
Classical Conversations
Classical Latin Schools
Classical Lutheran Schools
Institute for Catholic Liberal Education
Orthodox Christian Schools
Society for Classical Learning

PHILOSOPHY

8
What is the role of parents at classical Christian schools?

Children are a gift given to parents, not to schools, to responsibly raise in the ways of the LORD. God instructs parents to train up children in the way they should go in every area of life and during every stage of childhood. Therefore, parents are vitally important to the mission and vision of any educational institution. Classical Christian schools enter into a partnership with parents when a family joins a school. This partnership involves parents embracing and supporting the mission, leadership, and teachers at the school and the school employees communicating to parents throughout the formational education being provided.

9
What is the purpose of Christian education?

Christian education exists to pass down the truth of God's Word from one generation to the next, to inform students about all of God's created order, and - most importantly - to form students to be more like our LORD and Savior Jesus Christ. We know that a student will become like their teacher. So, this formation of students requires spiritually mature Christian teachers and school leaders who are excellent mentors and masters of their craft. Christian education also requires high academic and behavioral standards for excellence in education to occur. God uses teachers and school leaders to set the table for the Holy Spirit to work in the lives of the children attending Christian schools.

10
What is the purpose of classical education?

Classical education is designed as a great gift of western civilization to be passed down from one generation to the next. Each generation is responsible to entrust the next generation with the knowledge, traditions, and wisdom from the past. Our modern society is not uniquely independent from the past. It has been influenced by thousands of years of great scholars, philosophers, theologians, leaders, discoveries, and history. Western civilization is like a mighty river that has moved throughout time and the western world until it arrived at this present-day. The purpose of classical education is to fulfill our responsibility as citizens to entrust the traditions, culture, and wisdom of western civilization to our children.

11
Are students at classical Christian schools sheltered?

Children are appropriately protected from unnecessary and inappropriate exposure to the many social vices and immoral peer pressures found in many modern schools. However, this is not an effort to withdraw from society behind a fortress wall, but rather to create a greenhouse of controlled exposure while young children grow and mature. Students are purposefully exposed to both Christian and non-Christian ideas so that, like the trunks and roots of a tree in a greenhouse, their hearts and minds can grow strong and deeply rooted in the truth of God's Word. When students leave classical Christian schools, they are prepared with the skills to live courageously for Christ in a post-Christian society.

12
Why are students' affections an important part of education?

Training students to love the right things in a right way is a central component of classical Christian education. The cultivation of proper affections calibrates the hearts and minds of students to align with a love for what God loves and a hatred for what God hates. This proper formation and alignment of affections serve as a moral compass for graduates to serve as ethical Christian leaders, spouses, parents, and citizens throughout life.

13
What is the *western canon* of *great books?*

The great books are generally regarded as the time-tested foundational works of influential thought and history that have proven to be formational to western society. There are several closely overlapping lists that seek to create a definitive "western cannon" of about 500 books. The great books of western civilization have a renewed depth of meaning with each repeated reading, are applicable to contemporary society, and build to an understanding of the great ideas and questions of life.

14
Why is there a focus on reading the *great books?*

Reading the great books draws students into a discussion with the most brilliant minds of the past. This *great conversation* forces students to contemplate the big ideas of life's most important questions. While contemplating these great ideas, students are drawn into history and challenged to critically apply ideas from the past to the issues of today. The ideas found in the great books have influenced almost every aspect of modern-day western civilization. Understanding the origin and history of ideas can strengthen our understanding of current affairs and increase our wisdom as we live to glorify God each day.

15
Are anthologies used in classical Christian schools?

Classical schools do not use anthologies, or selected readings, as a structural base for curriculum. Instead, full original source texts are read, discussed, and compared to other original source documents. Reading the original thoughts and words of an author is highly preferred and valued over reading other people's interpretation of a text. This approach challenges students at classical Christian schools to engage with the original author in a way that requires critical thinking, analysis, synthesis, application, and knowledge of other subjects in order to fully comprehend and learn the material.

16
Is classical Christian education exclusive?

The design of classical Christian education is intended for every child and family to have access to this great curriculum, culture, and formational education. However, many families exclude themselves from the opportunity to be part of a classical Christian school. Some are not Christian and do not want a Christian education for their children, others are limited by an unwillingness to travel to a classical Christian school in their area, and many are not willing to pay for schooling that is "free" at the government schools. While classical Christian education is not intended to be exclusive, it often becomes exclusive.

The "exclusive" nature of a school simply means that families at the school have tightly aligned values, assumptions, and beliefs that are not shared by individuals not attending the school.

17
How is the arrangement of classes determined?

Classes at classical Christian schools are intentionally arranged in a way that promotes unity between subjects. The subject matter is often arranged so that literature, history, theology, art, and other classes are unified by covering similar time periods. History is often a determining factor in aligning and unifying the subjects being taught from year to year. It is also common for subjects to be unified by guiding questions or meta-questions that are thematic in nature each year. For example, a unifying theme for a year could examine justice, courage, or friendship.

18
Why is a liberal arts education important?

Liberal arts education has been proven to be an effective form of education that has stood the test of time for thousands of years. It is a form of education that brings freedom to individuals who would otherwise be bound by the limitations of ignorance. For this reason, liberal arts education is sometimes referred to as the liberating arts.

Individuals who have obtained a liberal arts education have the tools for lifelong learning and have the freedom to pursue any career. Liberal arts education is foundational to maintaining and advancing a free and democratic society.

CHRISTIAN

19
What is the role of the Bible in school?

The Bible is the foundation of any truly Christian school. The Bible informs every class, subject, handbook, administrative decision, event, and portrait of a graduate. If a school looks, feels, and operates like a government school with a Bible class added into the schedule, it is not operating as a truly intentional Christian school. It is commonplace for the Bible to be a natural part of discussions in every class, subject, and event at a classical Christian school. The Bible is the divinely inspired Word of God that is useful for teaching and training in righteousness. It is also the most influential text in the history of western civilization.

20
Do classical Christian schools teach evolution or creation?

Classical Christian schools teach that God created all things from nothing. This is a beautiful truth that is often difficult for our finite minds to conceive. Classical Christian schools believe the Bible is true, accurate, and reliable and teach students to believe the same. Everything (mathematics, science, the rise and fall of nations, language, etc.) is part of God's created order. Classical Christian education seeks to advance this interconnectivity and unity found in our Creator.

21
What is the role of Christian faith in education?

Christian faith is necessary for the full understanding of truth and any classical Christian education pursuing truth will naturally presuppose a belief in the Bible and faith in God. Therefore, the Christian faith of a student body is important to the educational process and contributes to a strong school culture which also increases the strength of the learning environment.

22
How are disagreements or offenses addressed?

In chapter 18 of the gospel of Matthew, Jesus instructs us to go directly to people who have offended us. This pattern of conflict resolution, established by Jesus, is used at classical Christian schools. If parents have a disagreement with each other, they are encouraged to work it out amongst themselves. In the same way, teachers and parents are encouraged to work through disagreements, before seeking to involve the administration. Finally, the head of school is the last point of appeal. Using this process, it should be extremely rare that a school board is ever involved with disagreements or offenses.

23
How is God discussed in school?

God describes Himself to us in the Bible as the sovereign authority of all things. He is also infinite, self-existing, eternal, unchangeable, omniscient, omnipresent, omnipotent, and so much more. Students are taught that God is the creator and sustainer of all things and that we, his created people, should live a life to glorify Him in all we do.

24
Do classical Christian schools support traditional marriage?

Marriage is a special covenant ordained by God to be entered into between one man and one woman. Students are taught that this is the only acceptable form of marriage ordained by God in the Bible. This design is for our good, the good of society, and the good of the earth.

25
Is homosexuality discussed in classical Christian schools?

Homosexuality, and all behavior under the LGBTQ label, are discussed as it arises naturally in classrooms. It is properly labeled as sin and students are instructed to resist this perversion and to guard their heart from it as they would all other sins. Students are also encouraged to lovingly call others out of this sin with the saving gospel message of faith in Jesus Christ.

26
Is abortion discussed at school?

Abortion is discussed as it naturally arises in classrooms and is taught as a sin. With the Bible as a sure foundation, classical Christian schools lead students to passages of scripture assuring them that God forms humans in the womb from the time of conception and that He ordains our days. The science of Biology also supports this truth. Students are also encouraged to lovingly care for others who are tempted toward abortion or who have been involved with abortion because there is hope and forgiveness found in Jesus Christ.

27
Is race and ethnicity discussed at school?

Christians understand that God creates all humans uniquely in his image and classical Christian schools do not emphasize skin color as an important distinction between humans. Instead, teachers point to passages of scripture clarifying that there are just two races of people. There are God's people and those that are not God's people. This is not a "color blind" approach. Instead, there is an emphasis on the truth that all humans are created in the image of God with equal intrinsic worth and value not linked to the amount of melanin in our skin, the country of our birth, or the culture in which we live.

28
Is there memorization of scripture?

Scripture memory is an important part of Christian education and should be expected and embraced by students of all ages and backgrounds. Memory work, especially the memorization of scripture, is an invaluable tool for any well-educated citizen in the kingdom of Christ. Memorization of scripture helps to hide God's Word in our hearts so that it can be used to bring clarity to our decisions and actions throughout our journey and path through life.

29
Are Bible classes part of the curriculum?

Bible classes are part of a Christian school curriculum. Studying the Bible is vitally important to the mission of Christian schools and classical Christian schools make a special effort to ensure that Theology and Bible instruction are not restricted to just one class. Instead, the Bible is integrated into every subject and is commonly referred to in class discussions in every subject.

30
How is discipline handled?

To foster Christian community with an environment conducive to learning, classical Christian schools have a handbook of rules, procedures, and guidelines. When students are not able to follow school rules, discipline is sometimes required. Discipline goes hand-in-hand with discipleship and students are mentored by a teacher or administrator who seeks to model the gospel for students. Students are taken through the steps of repentance, forgiveness, and restoration. Sometimes, there are consequences for an action, but many times students are fully restored after the three stages are covered through conversation and prayer.

31
Does mentoring take place in classical Christian schools?

Mentoring of students is an important part of the formational education provided in classical Christian schools. This mentoring includes teachers, staff, and peers. Teachers have an important role in the life of students and should not only seek to inform their minds academically, but also guide and mentor the worldview, speech, and actions of students in the school. Mentoring is not seen as going "above and beyond" the call of duty. Instead, it is an expectation of teachers at classical Christian schools as they partner with parents.

CLASSICAL

32
What is *in loco parentis?*

In loco parentis is a Latin phrase meaning "in the place of a parent." Teachers and administrators at classical Christian schools seek to live *in loco parentis* with students and parents choosing to attend the school. This involves a high level of trust and understanding from parents entering this partnership with schools. Parents are encouraged to trust that teachers and administrators approach this role seriously and should seek to support and encourage the school.

33
Why is *truth, goodness, and beauty* a common phrase?

Truth, goodness, and beauty are transcendental objective standards defined by, and found in God alone. Teachers lead students toward understanding, cultivating, and reflecting these virtues through a flourishing life. Students are taught to seek truth in all things, cultivate virtues of goodness, and reflect the beauty of our Savior. We must never tolerate a lie, never tolerate evil, and never tolerate misguided attempts at beauty while living a life for the good of others and the glory of God.

34
What is *multum non multa?*

Multum non multa is a Latin phrase meaning "much not many." This phrase is used to describe the philosophical approach of classical education. Classical schools expect students to learn deeply and thoroughly about the most important parts of western civilization. Learning *multum non multa* is different from most modern schools which seek to touch on many parts of subjects (like a rock skipping across a pond) without much depth in any of it.

35
What is *paideia?*

Paideia is an ancient Greek word meaning "the culture of a society." Educators in classical Christian schools understand that it is more than just knowledge being delivered to students at schools. The paideia of Christianity and western civilization is being passed down from one generation to the next generation through the curriculum, teachers, and community of classical Christian schools.

36
What is *ad fontes?*

Ad fontes is a Latin phrase meaning "to the sources." The preferred form of learning in classical Christian schools is from original sources rather than relying on textbooks, commentaries, or lectures. Reading the original source of an idea is fantastic but reading the original source in its original language is even better. This is one of the many reasons classical Christian schools require the study of ancient languages such as Latin, Greek, or Hebrew.

37
What are the *seven liberal arts*?

The seven liberal arts are Grammar, Logic, Rhetoric, Astronomy, Mathematics, Geometry, and Music. For the ancients, and throughout western civilization, these disciplines were thought of as essential areas of knowledge for any free person to flourish as a human and contribute fully to society as a citizen. These areas were codified as the seven liberal arts in late Roman antiquity and influenced the formation, foundation, and requirements of higher education.

38
What is the *Trivium*?

Grammar, Logic, and Rhetoric are the first three of the seven liberal arts and known as the Trivium. Each of these three are a stage of classical learning and employ a unique teaching methodology. Grammar covers the fundamentals or building blocks needed in all subjects and provides a firm foundation for future learning. Logic involves the critical thinking, reasoning, or why behind the subjects. Rhetoric focuses on expressing knowledge with poise, clarity, and wisdom when speaking or writing. Trivium means "three roads" in Latin which refers to these three ways of learning.

39
What is the *Quadrivium*?

Mathematics, Geometry, Astronomy, and Music are the second half of the seven liberal arts and known as the *Quadrivium*. These are known as the upper division of the seven liberal arts and were the majority of the medieval university curriculum. The *Quadrivium* was designed to build on the Trivium and draw students into higher order reasoning and interaction with the cosmos. Now, schools around the nation integrate these disciplines into earlier stages of education to foster a greater unity of learning and interplay between the arts and sciences.

40
What is meant by *plundering the Egyptians*?

Classical Christian schools study the best and brightest scholars from both the Christian and non-Christian world. During this process, there is an intentional effort to take every thought captive for the glory of God. This requires teachers to lead students through a process of sifting material to take what is praiseworthy and leave behind what is not true, good, or beautiful. This process is referred to as "plundering the Egyptians" to take and learn from the best of ancient cultures.

41
What is meant by *Scholé* in education?

Scholé is a Greek word meaning "leisure." In Latin this word is *scola* and in English it is school. The idea of restful learning, or learning as leisure, is an important concept in education. Schools were not designed as job training or a platform from which to launch students into economic gain. Education should lead students toward becoming more fully human. Time for contemplation should be baked into the fabric of a school. This form of learning is not lazy. It is intentional, disciplined, and focused on the true end of education. This *scholé*, or leisurely approach to learning allows for long-term comprehension and lifetime formation of students.

42
What is meant by teaching students *how* to think not *what* to think?

It is the desire of classical Christian schools to create lifelong learners. To do this, students need to be given tools for learning that they can use for life. Giving students the tools needed for lifelong learning is far better than teaching students lists of facts during a lecture. Some of the many tools that students are given are reading, writing, Latin, critical thinking (Logic), communication (Rhetoric), etiquette, biblical knowledge, a biblical worldview, and many other skills.

43
What is meant by *joining the great conversation?*

Some conversations last six minutes, some last six days, and some last six thousand years. Students at classical Christian schools join in a conversation that was started thousands of years ago. Reading ancient texts from theologians like Augustine, philosophers like Aristotle, scholars like Euclid, historians like Herodotus, and storytellers like Homer allows students to pull up a chair to be part of the great conversation about the most important questions in life. Engaging in a conversation with the greatest minds of the western world allows students to gain a deep understanding of reoccurring patterns and themes in western civilization and are then uniquely poised to offer solutions to current challenges facing modern society.

44
What does it mean to *cultivate virtue* in students?

Just as students grow in their ability to read and write, students can also grow in virtue. A virtuous life involves knowledge, belief, and action for the good of others and the glory of God. Becoming more virtuous allows humans to flourish by fulfilling the purpose for which they were created. Cultivating an environment, culture, and programs for students to intentionally grow in virtue is a challenging task but an important role of true education.

45
What does the term *soul formation* mean?

Every human is created with a soul that will last forever. With this in mind, classical Christian schools know that the soul formation involved in educating the whole student will have eternal benefit. It is not the role of the school to save souls (only God can do that), but teachers, administrators, and other individuals serving at schools are used by God to set the table for the Holy Spirit to work in the life of students and the recalibration of the soul toward the truth, goodness, and beauty of our triune God.

46
What is *omnibus* in a curriculum?

The term *omnibus* refers to the ability to provide for many things at once. In classical Christian schools, *omnibus* refers to a class in the upper school that is designed to teach literature, history, and theology in a well-designed and unified structure. *Omnibus* classes are a practical way to advance the desire for unity in learning rather than disunity often created by teaching unique and non-integrated subjects.

47
What does *imago dei* mean?

Imago dei is a Latin phrase meaning "image of God." This phrase is used as a theological term that denotes the unique qualities of humans (as compared to the earth, plants, and animals) the special relationship humans have with God, and the responsibility humans have to reflect God in life.

48
What does *ex nihilo* mean?

Ex nihilo is a Latin phrase meaning "creation out of nothing." This phrase is used as a theological term to explain that matter is not eternal and was created by our eternal God. Only God is eternal, and all things in heaven and on earth were created *ex nihilo*.

49
What does *Soli Deo Gloria* mean?

Soli Deo Gloria is a Latin phrase meaning "glory to God alone." This single phrase best encompasses the desire of classical Christian educators. Classical Christian schools do not exist for test scores, championships, prestige, politics, or fame. Instead, they exist for the glory of God alone.

50
What does the word *arete* mean?

Arete is a Greek word meaning "excellence." In ancient Greek culture, the term *arete* was used most often to refer to *moral virtue* or the *fulfillment of purpose*. In classical Christian schools, it is used in this same way to refer to the cultivation of excellence and virtue in students in the hopes that they will fulfill the purpose God has for them in life.

GRAMMAR

51
Is Grammar a subject or a stage of education?

Grammar is a formal subject of study and a stage of classical education. The subject of grammar focuses on learning words, parts of speech, and the construction of ideas into meaningful sentences. Every subject has a grammar or foundational knowledge that is essential to master before moving into a deeper study of the subject. For example, there is a grammar of math, a grammar of history, a grammar of music, and a grammar of the Bible. The grammar stage of classical Christian education takes place in the youngest grades (K-5 or K-6) and focuses on students learning the fundamentals, or grammar, of every subject so that they are prepared for a lifetime of learning.

52
Why are songs, chants, and memorization so important?

Children learn differently at every stage of development. Young children can typically memorize more efficiently than older children. So, in the early years of classical Christian education, students memorize amazing amounts of information like multiplication tables, states and capitals, history timelines, Bible verses, scientific categorization, and so much more. When information is set to music or chants, retention of new information becomes even easier, and the information is likely to be retained for life.

53
Why do students memorize so many things?

Memorization helps students recall information, but it also strengthens the brain and prepares students for more difficult forms of learning and the ability to retain a greater volume of information throughout every stage of the educational process. Memorization expands memory related portions of the brain, improves the functionality of memory recall, and increases overall creativity.

54
Why is cursive taught?

Multiple studies have shown that cursive writing increases learning levels and cognitive abilities by training the brain to integrate visual, tactile, and fine motor skills simultaneously. It also increases connectivity between the right and left hemispheres of the brain. Cursive handwriting activates the same regions of the brain that is used when reading, but this area is not activated by typing. Writing in cursive also increases spelling abilities and has been shown to be helpful to students with learning differences such as dyslexia and dysgraphia. Finally, being able to read original documents such as the Declaration of Independence is always helpful to a classically educated student seeking to read original source material.

55
Why is the study of Latin important?

Latin is a difficult language to study and requires students to learn logical reasoning, perseverance, and patience at an early age. More importantly, approximately fifty percent of the English language comes from Latin and studying it greatly advances the understanding of our own language. Latin is also the origin of the romance languages of Spanish, Portuguese, French, Italian, and Romanian. Students who have studied Latin can learn these languages with greater ease as they get older. Students who have studied Latin are also more prepared for advanced studies in legal, medical, and other Latin-based disciplines. Finally, the study of Latin increases national standardized test scores and scores on college entrance exams.

56
Why is phonics used to learn reading?

Letters and letter combinations represent a variety of sounds in the English language. These sounds are used to produce words. Children who master phonetic sounds will be able to accurately read almost any word they encounter. This is a powerful ability and a fundamental building block of a lifetime of learning and knowledge acquisition. Systematic phonics instruction has been repeatedly shown to be the best approach to teaching children to read. Students who do not master phonograms may have reading difficulties throughout life.

57
Why is proper spelling emphasized?

Proper spelling is directly correlated with phonetic awareness and is an essential tool for written communication and reading. Spelling is often a struggle for some students but is a vitally important tool to master at a young age.

58
Why do students study ancient history at such a young age?

The study of history is a very important part of classical Christian education. Students cover the history of western civilization from creation to present two or three times throughout a K-12 scope and sequence. Each time a student cycles through studying a period of history there will be an opportunity for a greater depth of learning and a more profound understanding of it. In the grammar stage students generally study creation, ancient Egypt, Greece, Rome, and the ensuing time periods that build on each other chronologically from year to year. This systematic approach gives students a deep understanding of the world and the historic traditions that have influenced modern western culture.

LOGIC

59
Is Logic a subject or a stage of education?

Logic is a formal subject of study and a stage of classical education. The subject of logic focuses on the study of reason, principals, criteria, and valid inferences toward the determination and expression of truth. As a subject, most classical Christian schools study informal and formal logic as a specific subject in grade seven or eight. The logic stage of education takes place in the middle school (grades 6-9) and focuses on improving critical thinking. Logic comes from the Greek word *logos* and encompasses words, thoughts, ideas, arguments, reason, and integrity. Many schools refer to this stage as dialectic rather than logic.

60
Why is the study of logic so important?

Critical thinking and common sense are uncommon in modern society. The study of formal and informal logic is a major part of improving critical thinking and reasoning. These skills improve scientific reasoning, conducting lab experiments, performing mathematical functions, academic writing, verbal communication, debate, journalism, and a host of other activities. The study of logic also allows students to spot fallacies and incongruent reasoning during discussions, in the news, or when reading articles.

61
Why are questions a major tool of teachers in the logic school?

Children learn differently at every stage of development. Young adults in the pre-teen and early teenage years begin to question almost everything as they test foundational learning from their time in grammar school. Teachers use this desire and "cut with the grain" by asking questions and seeking to answer questions while instructing students in the logic school. Life can seem unstable or confusing during this stage of maturing into adulthood, but students at classical Christian schools are given the opportunity to participate in the learning process and develop critical thinking skills while embodying knowledge through question-based learning.

62
Is it common for children to act rude or mean in logic school?

Many parents become concerned when their children begin to act out, struggle with peer relationships, or adopt new inappropriate patterns of behavior during middle school. It can be difficult to understand the thoughts, desires, and actions of children during this time. However, by consistently addressing bad behavior with increased love and patience, children will typically move through this stage of development within a few years. School employees have great experience from working with hundreds of students at this age and want to encourage and help parents and children. When students become argumentative at this age, classical Christian schools teach them how to argue logically, truthfully, and respectfully.

63
Why is ancient history a focus of study?

The study of ancient history allows students to understand major events that have shaped current reality. Learning the causes and effects of historic events also allows students to learn from the past so that they are informed with the knowledge and wisdom to guide western civilization as good citizens in the future. It has been said that politics is downstream from culture, but both are downstream from history and ancient history is the wellspring that eventually led to modern society.

64
Why is ancient literature a focus of study?

Reading the greatest books ever written is an important part of classical Christian education. Ancient literature allows students to be transported to another time, place, and culture. This transportation through literature awakens wonder and imagination in students. It also provides an opportunity for students to connect with people who are unlike them and going through experiences they have never encountered. These experiences foster an understanding about the human experience and an opportunity for growth and maturity without ever physically leaving our own town or schools.

65
Why are false gods and mythology part of the curriculum?

Religion and objects of worship are an integral part of every culture. The ancient Egyptians, Greeks, and Romans were polytheistic (worshiped many gods), but the Hebrews and Christians were monotheistic (worshiped one God). This caused great tensions and resulted in persecution and wars. Students cannot fully understand history, literature, art, and the Bible without a knowledge of the false gods and mythology promoted in pagan cultures. The apostle Paul also makes it clear that Jesus is the true fulfillment of the many false myths and gods found throughout history. Learning to see these patterns in history helps students to see the false gods and myths presented as truth in our current culture.

66
Why is physical education required?

Physical activity improves learning and prepares students to actively use their body as part of being a fully formed human. The ancient Greeks understood the importance of developing the body as an equal component to the academic training of the mind and soul and Plato founded his academy at a gymnasium. God has given humans a body, mind, and spirit and development in all three of these areas is important. Focusing only on the mind, or knowledge, can tempt students to believe that the body is unimportant. This type of thinking led to the heresy of Gnosticism.

RHETORIC

67
Is Rhetoric a subject or a stage of education?

Rhetoric is a formal subject of study and a stage of classical education. The study of rhetoric teaches students the art of written and oral communication. Excellent rhetorical skills allow students to express the knowledge, faith, wisdom, and virtue they have gained while at the academy. Opportunities for students to grow in rhetorical skills are woven throughout the K-12 curriculum and formal rhetoric classes often occur in the last two years before graduation. The rhetoric stage of education occurs during high school (grades 9-12). During this stage, students are encouraged to actively participate in the teaching process and classroom discussions.

68
Why is art a required subject?

Our God is the creator of all things and our ultimate inspiration and source of what it means to create true, good, and beautiful art. Art classes teach students to cultivate artistic talents, reflect the image of God, cultivate an aesthetic awareness, and appreciate beauty, art, and artists. Cultivating creativity develops the use of portions of the brain that are not often engaged during other classes and help to develop more fully formed humans.

69
Why is music a required subject?

Music is one of the seven liberal arts and is a very important area of study for classical Christian students. Studying music fosters analytic thinking and singing in parts promotes Christian unity. There have been many studies correlating music education with positive impacts on brain function, hand-eye coordination, attention span, learning languages, math, creativity, and social skills. More importantly, music was given to us by God to praise Him each week with fellow believers and throughout our week. This is one skill that students will use forever to praise God in the new heaven and new earth.

70
What is a house system?

The use of house systems has become popular at many classical Christian schools in recent years. The house system was originally developed and used at boarding schools in England and Wales. House systems in American K-12 schools place students into groups, or houses, to foster leadership, mentoring, service, friendships, and community to advance the mission of a school and making a large group seem smaller. Some classical Christian schools use the house system for the full school while others use it only in grades 6-8, 7-12 or 9-12.

71
Why is technology not emphasized?

Technology is used as a tool to advanced learning and organizational efficiency but is never used to replace original source texts or teachers. Cell phones and other technology distracting from Christian community, school culture, and education are not permitted to be used during school. Personalized instruction from master teachers who care about students is the preferred way of learning at classical Christian schools.

72
What is Socratic Learning?

Socrates (470 - 399 B.C.) was a Greek philosopher who is well known for leading students to deep understanding of knowledge through the constant use of questions. Teachers at classical Christian schools often use this technique, referred to as Socratic discussions, to draw students into deeper learning and understanding of truth. By actively participating in the learning and teaching process students master the subject being studied. It is noteworthy that Socrates instructed Plato, Plato taught Aristotle, and Aristotle tutored Alexander the Great.

73
What is the role of athletics?

Athletics are a co-curricular activity and help to foster the educational process of students outside of the classroom. Physical activity improves learning and prepares students to actively use their body as part of being a fully formed human. The ancient Greeks understood the importance of developing the body as an equal component to the academic training of the mind and soul and Plato founded his academy at a gymnasium. God has created humans with a body, mind, and spirit and the development of all three areas is important. Focusing only on the mind, or knowledge, can tempt students to believe that the body is unimportant. This type of thinking led to the heresy of Gnosticism.

74
Are classical Christian schools weak in math and science?

In the early 1990's many newly formed classical Christian schools were not as strong in math and science as they were in the humanities. Now math and science have become very strong at classical Christian schools. Graduates usually score much higher on college entrance exams than their state and national government school counterparts. More importantly, these subjects are taught from a Christian worldview.

75
Why is Greek a valuable language to study?

About thirty percent of English words come from Greek and learning Greek can help us to better understand English. The study of Koine Greek (ancient Greek) can also help students to read original source material. The New Testament was written in Greek and students who have studied this ancient language can deeply study God's Word and the nuances of the original text. There are also many other important ancient documents composed in Greek.

76
How are students trained in proper manners?

Students are trained in poise, eloquence, and etiquette through formal and informal instruction. Faculty and staff require proper manners and decorum in classrooms and hallways to ensure a safe and orderly environment that fosters an excellent educational setting for student learning. This is the informal process by which students develop proper manners. Students also receive formal instruction on ways to properly behave at various social events, addressing adults or dignitaries, setting a table, dancing at weddings, and more. This instruction helps to fosters a civil society.

77
What is a senior thesis presentation?

Many classical Christian schools require students to deliver a public oral presentation of a major research paper toward the end of their senior year. A committee of teachers or other experts in the field of research often review or judge the paper and presentation. This process helps with the solidification of written and verbal rhetorical skills that or are a hallmark of classical Christian education.

PARENTING

78
How can I support the school?

Parents can support the school through prayer, patience, communication, encouragement, talent, and finances. Praying for the staff and students is a blessing to the school. Education is a long, hard, and often messy process that requires patience with everyone involved. Encouraging teachers in their efforts and encouraging children to work hard during difficult times is very beneficial to the culture of the school and the long-term success of students. Using talents to volunteer to serve at the school is always needed and greatly appreciated. Financial support is helpful to advancing the mission of the school and keeping tuition affordable. Financial support includes paying tuition on time as well as the giving of financial donations.

79
How can I help my child with Latin?

The best way to help a child with Latin is to learn it with them. This will encourage them as you model how to be a lifelong learner and you will also be able to help with daily lessons. If you do not have the opportunity to learn Latin with your child, it is imperative that you speak highly about the value of learning this language. Use phrases such as: "It's so great that you are learning Latin." "Latin is a cool secret language." "Make sure you review your Latin a little every night." "Can you teach me a little Latin?" Students who struggle in Latin often have parents who complain about it in front of their children as a "useless" or "unimportant" part of the curriculum that they must "tolerate."

80
What type of students thrive in classical Christian schools?

Hard working and joyful students with supportive parents that value education and are deeply committed to the Christian faith tend to thrive in classical Christian schools while students who are unmotivated to learn, frequently complain about teachers, and make excuses for poor results tend to struggle academically or socially.

81
Why are there so many rules for students?

A structured and orderly classroom and school produces an excellent learning environment for students. School rules provide students with clear expectations and a pathway for success. School rules also provide students the opportunity to develop self-control, humility, respect, patience, and many other important and beneficial characteristics.

82
Why are uniforms worn by students?

School uniforms are a great way to provide unity, eliminate distractions, and foster safety. Sport teams, police departments, militaries, and other organizations all use uniforms to increase unity. Uniforms also provide a safe environment by allowing staff to identify non-students easily and quickly. Finally, uniforms eliminate distracting clothing and increase the academic learning environment.

83
Why is there such a big focus on cultivating virtue?

True education goes beyond gaining academic knowledge and includes the formation of the whole student. Ancient philosophers, the founders of America, and the Bible all advocate the importance of cultivating virtue as a central component of a flourishing human. The Bible teaches us to supplement our faith with virtue and Aristotle promoted a life of virtue as the only true way to achieve happiness in life. For Christian, American, or school culture to succeed, we need virtuous citizens. Classical Christian schools take virtue formation seriously and look for ways to model it, discuss it, and foster opportunities for virtuous actions.

84
How can I find a classical Christian school near me?

It is actually quite simple to find a classical Christian school located near you. Simply go to the websites of the organizations listed in Question 7 and look for the map of member school locations. If you can not find one within one hour of your home, consider finding a few likeminded families and starting a classical Christian school or co-op in your area.

85
What books should I read for a deeper understanding of classical Christian education?

The Lost Tools of Learning: by Dorothy Sayers
The Abolition of Man: by C.S. Lewis
A Case for Classical Education: by Douglas Wilson
The Liberal Arts Tradition: by Kevin Clark and Ravi Jain
The Well-Trained Mind: by S. Wise Bauer and J. Wise
Beauty in the World: by Stratford Caldecott
Wisdom and Eloquence: by Littlejohn and Evans
An Introduction to Classical Education: by C. Perrin
The Core: by Leigh Bortins

GRADUATES

86
Are students prepared for college?

Graduates are well prepared for college and will typically have many options and scholarships from which to choose. Students matriculate into the fields of medicine, math, law, business, education, engineering, media, fine arts, and any other area to which they feel called. Average standardized test scores for graduates are often much higher than state and national averages, but high-test scores and college are not the aim of classical Christian schools. The goal is to cultivate human flourishing in students. The excellent knowledge, belief, and actions of graduates allows them to confidently master any college program or job as part of a wholistic life that glorifies God.

87
Are graduates prepared for a job?

Graduates of classical Christian schools are well prepared to step directly into a career after graduation. A liberal arts education develops a strong work ethic, critical thinking, and excellent communication skills required in the work force. Many graduates will quickly find opportunities for promotions and leadership resulting from a recognition of these skills that are fostered and honed at classical Christian schools.

88
What are the characteristics of an ideal classical Christian school graduate?

The best graduates of classical Christian schools are typically involved in their local church, love the LORD, find ways to serve at school and in the local community, love reading deeply and on a variety of topics, and have a deep desire to learn and grow. They speak and write well, think logically, and have a biblical Christ-centered worldview. They have strongly developed the virtues of gratitude, humility, joy, perseverance, and courage.

89
Do graduates remain committed to the Christian faith as adults?

Graduates from classical Christian schools present a stronger commitment to the Christian faith than Christian students attending other types of schools. Dan Smithwick led the way in researching this area with the PEERS test. Timothy Dernlan confirmed Smithwick's research through an independent quantitative study comparing classical and non-classical Christian school students in the areas of biblical knowledge, belief, and action. Most recently, Cardis partnered with the University of Notre Dame to produce the Good Soil Report. This research surveyed the practices, beliefs, and other outcomes of alumni ranging from ages twenty-four to forty-four. While only God can produce Christian faith, classical Christian schools are clearly cultivating good soil from which Christian faith and commitment can grow strong and lead to a flourishing Christian life.

GOVERNMENT

90
Are classical charter schools Christian?

Charter schools in America are simply an alternative form of government schools and are not permitted to advance Christianity or any other religion. Many classical charter schools seek to educate good moral citizens but lack the ability to fully form flourishing Christians because the truth, goodness, and beauty of God's Word is not the foundation of charter school education.

91
Do classical Christian schools accept vouchers?

Most classical Christian schools have seen the great wisdom of not accepting vouchers or any other funding tied to the strings of government control and regulations. Schools accepting vouchers or federal funds are at a much higher risk of government intrusion than those not accepting these funds. Institutions that do accept vouchers, state funding, federal funding, or government sponsored educational savings plans will often have strict safeguards in place to protect the religious freedoms of the school.

92

Who were some of the main influences on modern government schools?

Modern education can be traced to theorists like Rousseau, Dewey, and Piaget. These educational reformers worked to dilute and remove Christian worldview from American education. Rousseau promoted moral education through social experiences rather than religious instruction. Piaget greatly promoted child-centered education and a segmented learning structure that advanced disunity rather than unified wholistic learning. Dewey turned away from an early influence of Christian education after being drawn to the work of eighteen century German philosopher Hegel. Dewey promoted truth as scientifically mediated knowledge and wrote about the need for the Church to be usurped by democracy and human experiential learning.

93

How did Rousseau, Dewey, Piaget, and other modern philosophers influence modern schools?

By the early 1900's Christian influence had been systematically removed from American education and replaced with moral teachings and a secular worldview. This paved the way for progressive post-Christian doctrine to be easily incorporated into the daily curriculum and learning outcomes of government schools. First, science became the new religion that filled the void left by the removal of Christianity. Recently, the religion of progressive socialism packaged as self-selected sexual identity, critical race theory, economic human capitol, and other progressive agendas of indoctrination that place human feelings above God's truth have taken hold of the vacuum created by modern educational theorists. Progressive non-Christian ideology is now prevalent in government schools and influential at many modern private schools.

94
Are classical Christian schools certified by the government?

Most classical Christian schools reject all state and government funds. This allows for independence from government regulations and mandates that continue to have adverse effects on children seeking to learn in government schools. Classical Christian schools are operated under local independent school boards and administrators specifically focused on advancing best practice for classical Christian education. Many schools also hold national accreditation through established and recognized associations and organizations (see Question 7 for partial list).

95
Do classical Christian school teachers hold credentials or teacher certification?

Many teachers and administrators at classical Christian schools do not hold government certifications or licenses. Such programs are designed to advance a form, method, and mission of education that is antithetical to the vision of classical Christian education. Instead, teachers at classical Christian schools are held to a higher standard and the absence of unions allows schools to effectively retain only the best teachers who most effectively advance student learning and formation. There are also several programs through classical Christian school organizations that allow teachers to hold national certifications and endorsements specifically designed for classical Christian educators.

QUOTES

96
What did Plato say about education?

No man should bring children into the world who is unwilling to persevere to the end in their nature and education.

The object of education is to teach us to love what is beautiful.

To love rightly is to love what is orderly and beautiful in an educated and disciplined way.

Seek truth while you are young, or if you do not, it will later escape your grasp.

What then is the education to be? I believe in gymnastics for the body and music for the mind.

97
What did Aristotle say about education?

Educating the mind without educating the heart is no education at all.

All who have meditated on the art of governing mankind have been convinced that the fate of empires depends on the education of youth.

The best way to teach morality is to make it a habit with children.

The habits we form from childhood make no small difference, but rather they make all the difference.

All youth should also be educated with music and physical education.

98
What did G.K. Chesterton say about education?

Education is simply the soul of a society as it passes from one generation to another.

The purpose of Compulsory Education is to deprive the common people of their commonsense.

Without education we are in a horrible and deadly danger of taking educated people seriously.

Education is not a subject, and it does not deal in subjects. It is instead the transfer of a way of life.

99
What did C.S. Lewis say about education?

Education without values, as useful as it is, seems rather to make man a more clever devil.

The task of the modern educator is not to cut down jungles, but to irrigate deserts.

If education is beaten by training (for a job), civilization dies.

The basic proposal of the new (modern) education is to be that dunces and idlers must not be made to feel inferior to intelligent and industrious pupils.

100
What have others said about education?

I am much afraid that schools will prove to be the great gates of hell unless they diligently labor in explaining the Holy Scriptures, engraving them in the hearts of youth.
- Martin Luther

The great defect of our education today (is that) we fail lamentably on the whole in teaching them how to think.
- Dorothy Sayers

Education is the key to unlock the golden door of freedom.
- George Washington Carver

It was a mistake for evangelical Christians to believe that anything other than a Christian education is safe.
- Albert Mohler

The end of learning is to repair the ruins of our first parents by regaining to know God aright, and out of that knowledge to love him, to imitate him, to be like him.
- John Milton

Intelligence plus character is the goal of true education.
- Martin Luther King Jr.

The mind is not a vessel to be filled, but a fire to be kindled.
- Plutarch

The main hope of a nation lies in the proper education of it to youth.

- Erasmus

Education has produced a vast population able to read but unable to distinguish what is worth reading.

- G.M. Trevelyan

The most important Christian education institution is not the pulpit or the school... it is the Christian family, and that institution has to a very large extent ceased to do its work.

- J. Gresham Machen

CONCLUSION

The modern mind often makes it difficult to fully embrace everything required of students, parents, and teachers pursuing excellence in classical Christian education. However, there is a rich history and well-reasoned philosophy undergirding this great form of education. The classical and Christian approach to education is most effective when it is fully embraced as a way of life. It should not be viewed as a silver bullet, guarantee of success, or add on to an otherwise modern lifestyle.

Parents and teachers must create a variety of learning opportunities for students and encourage them to cultivate a passion for learning, an ever-increasing faith, and virtuous actions that may sometimes seem odd to peers who have been seduced by our modern post-Christian culture. Continue to be thoughtful and intentional about seemingly small details of life as you influence, guide, and pass on the Christian faith and western traditions to the next generation through a classical Christian way of life.

May God bless you and keep you as you seek to advance classical Christian education for the good of society and the glory of God.

Truth, Goodness, and Beauty
are objective standards defined by and found in God alone.
Let us never tolerate a lie, never tolerate evil, and
never tolerate misguided attempts at beauty
as we live to glorify God.

- Timothy Dernlan

REFERENCES

Anthony, M. J., & Benson, W. S. (2003). *Exploring the history and philosophy of Christian education: Principles for the 21st century.* Grand Rapids, MI: Kregel.

Bauer, S. W., & Wise, J. (2009). *The well-trained mind: A guide to the classical education at home.* New York, NY: W.W. Norton & Company.

Brainy Quote. (2019). Retrieved August 15 - December 22, 2019, from https://www.brainyquote.com.

Crossway Bibles. (2007). *ESV: Study Bible: English standard version.* Wheaton, Ill: Crossway Bibles.

Littlejohn, R., & Evans, C. T. (2006). *Wisdom and eloquence: A Christian paradigm for classical learning.* Wheaton, IL: Crossway Books.

Nehemiah Institute. (2012). *Peers testing.* Retrieved from http://www.nehemiahinstitute.com/peers.php

Perrin, C. A. (2004). *An introduction to classical education: A guide for parents.* Harrisburg, PA: Classical Academic Press.

Sayers, D. L. (1947). The lost tools of learning. *The National Review, 7*(1), 237-244.

Veith Jr., G. E., & Kern, A. (2001). *Classical education: The movement sweeping America.* Washington, DC: Capital Research Center.

Wilson, D. (2003). *The case for classical Christian education.* Wheaton, IL: Crossway Books.

ABOUT THE AUTHOR

Dr. Timothy Dernlan is an author, consultant, speaker, and visionary Christian school leader. He is passionate about advancing Christian community and culture through education. He taught theater, math, rhetoric, physical education, personal finance, leadership, communication, and systematic theology before turning his focus to school leadership.

Much of his early life was influenced by the sport of wrestling. He won All-American honors while at Purdue University, represented the United States as an athlete at the Jr. World Championships, Pan American Championships, and competed in the 2000 and 2004 final Olympic Trials. He coached at Purdue, Ohio State, Penn State, Lehigh, and Ashland University and was named the NCAA Midwest Region Coach of the Year in 2008.

Dr. Dernlan has served as headmaster, head of school, and superintendent of Christian schools ranging in size from 200 to 1300 students. Dernlan and his wife were married in 2000 and have four children.

MORE INFORMATION

www.TimDernlan.com

www.ClassicalChristianEducation.org

Made in the USA
Columbia, SC
08 August 2022

64873944R10046